Understand

Point, Evidence, and

Explanation (PEE)

Edited by Lana Davies

Passing your GCSE's with flying colours is the primary focus of every high school student (and if not, it should be). Getting super grades will help you to get into the College of your choice and open up many doors for you in the long run is something we've been told for years, and that is TRUE!

Now, examiners are taking this one step further and actively encouraging students to re-sit important subjects such as Maths and English and even threatening to remove funding for those in further education, should they fail.

So, this short book has been designed to help you succeed in a core subject which is considered to be one of the essential qualifications to be looked at by Colleges, Universities, and Employers around the world.

Understanding Point, Evidence, and Explanation (PEE)

GCSE English covers a broad range of sections such as looking at fiction, non-fiction, comparison of texts, poetry, and spelling, punctuation, and grammar. However, we will focus on one part of the English which is writing.

Writing is a huge part of being able to thrive in a GCSE English exam (whether Literature or Language), and we will be looking at how to master this skill using the famous and widely recognized PEE (Point, Evidence, Explanation) method.

Whether you're looking to sit your GCSE's in a few months or a few years, we have broken down the PEE method for you to ace any writing task before you.

> **Note:** The PEE method is also sometimes referred to as PEED (Point, Evidence, Technique, Explain, Reader) or PEEL (Point, Evidence, Explain, Link) which can also be used as an extension to the PEE method. This method is mainly used to add more depth to our 'Explanation' and linking back to the original question although we will look to cover how you can do this with the PEE method.

If you have been taught using the PEED or PEEL method at School, then I recommend continuing to use that method using the points we cover.

Understanding Point, Evidence, and Explanation (PEE)

So what is the PEE all about?

PEE (Point, Evidence, Explanation {or explain}) is an essay writing technique used in English. It is a format that helps you to write an essay effectively, a paragraph, a thesis statement to enable you to answer questions correctly and adequately. Interestingly, it also helps to assess reading. This book is about the concept of PEE being used in diverse ways, why we use it, along with examples of how to use it as well as looking at other key points when writing.

We will follow the following guide when compiling this book:

- Introduction to PEE
- Writing a response: PEE
- PEE chain
- PEE examples
- Things to consider before you start writing
- Introduction to writing
- Extended PEE examples
- Where else can we use PEE paragraphs?
- Checking first drafts of work
- Literature and Argument Essays (PEE)
- Final Note

Understanding Point, Evidence, and Explanation (PEE)

What exactly does PEE mean?

Point – Here, you would need to sum up the main point from the text.

You can introduce your point by using phrases such as:

- In my opinion...
- In the extract, the writer uses...
- The writer uses...
- Similarly...
- Firstly...
- Secondly...
- Both...
- In contrast...
- One of the language features used is....

An example is: *"In my opinion, girls should be encouraged to be feminists."*

Evidence - The quote selected from the text to prove or support what you are saying. Here, you are raising this evidence to assist the point you raised earlier.

You can introduce your evidence by using phrases such as:

- For example, the author says...
- An example of this is...
- In Line 13, Dickens highlights...

Understanding Point, Evidence, and Explanation (PEE)

- This is shown when...
- This can be seen...
- This is demonstrated when it states...
- We know this because it says...
- The evidence for this is...

An example: *This shows when the author states, "Men get drunk and thereby, turn their wives into punching bags."*

> **Note:** Try not to make your evidence too long and do not go over a maximum of 15 words for your evidence. Having too many words as your evidence means you can have words/phrases that are unrelated to your point which examiners don't like.

Explanation - A more detailed description of the point and personal opinion of the writer. Here, you justify the point and evidence. You explain how the evidence raised justifies the point earlier raised.

This is a CRUCIAL part of your paragraph to gaining higher marks. An in-depth response with original interpretations in this part can really make a difference to your overall grade.

Ask yourself:

Why is the quotation significant? What effect does it have on the reader? Why has the writer used this technique?

Understanding Point, Evidence, and Explanation (PEE)

You can introduce your explanation by using words such as:

- This shows...
- This suggests...
- This implies...
- This is effective because...
- The writer has chosen this technique because...
- This would make the reader feel this has been used because...

An example: *The writer uses repetition to describe the authors of the previous generations. This is shown when it says, "Everything was boring, Shakespeare was boring, and Dickens was boring." This shows the students had little interest in reading any classical books. The repetition of the word "boring" illustrates the current students are disengaged with the books of the past and Mr. Walsh should consider finding modern books to spark an interest in books again. For an advocate of ancient literature such as Mr. Walsh, we can understand his disappointment with the current crop of students.*

> Task!
> Cover the answer below, read the following passage and answer the question that follows:

"I am Jill, and this is my story. I was a normal schoolgirl whose life revolved around school and home alone. However, ever since I moved into this boarding school, things have changed. I no longer have the time to engage in some extracurricular

Understanding Point, Evidence, and Explanation (PEE)

activities of my choice; instead, I'm stuck with playing basketball and other games that I find boring. Every blessed day, I offer prayers to God to make my parents suddenly change their mind and withdraw me from this school. The girl whose bed is next to mine is named Janet. She annoys me at any slight moment. I find her particularly annoying, not only because of her looks but because she doesn't even attempt to look as good as me. I heard someone whispering that she came from the slum. I cannot believe that I've been sharing my room with someone from the slum. No wonder she stinks so badly. I wish school would be over soon so that I could get back to my normal way of life and my princess lifestyle."

After reading the passage, do you consider Jill as a proud young girl?

Answer:

We can see from the extract Jill is a very proud young girl. This was demonstrated in her statement, "I cannot believe that I've been sharing my room with someone from the slum." Her statement here suggests how irritating she finds her roommate. She waits anxiously for school to be over so that she can get back to her "princess" lifestyle.

The above answer is an effortless way to write out your PEE.

However, this answer can easily be developed.

Understanding Point, Evidence, and Explanation (PEE)

Task!
Have a go at expanding the above explanation to develop this answer. Think about:

- How the evidence makes us feel about Jill.
- Why this quotation is significant.

Note: Writing out a PEE paragraph does not need to be long, and you can complete your point effectively with just a few sentences.

Understanding Point, Evidence, and Explanation (PEE)

Looking beyond PEE...

You may have come across this common picture in your English lessons at School showing you the table you should be looking to follow. This is a practical ladder showing you how to progress with your writing and to achieve a fitting answer. You should be looking to reach the top of the ladder (Evaluate) to feel like you've analyzed thoroughly.

> **Note:** The goals of PEE, PEEL, PEED, and PEEDL are to encourage you to write a complete and thorough answer which shows examiners you understand EXACTLY what the question is asking and that you can demonstrate excellent writing skills.

Please take some moments to revise the steps of this ladder later on to refresh your understanding of the PEE writing process.

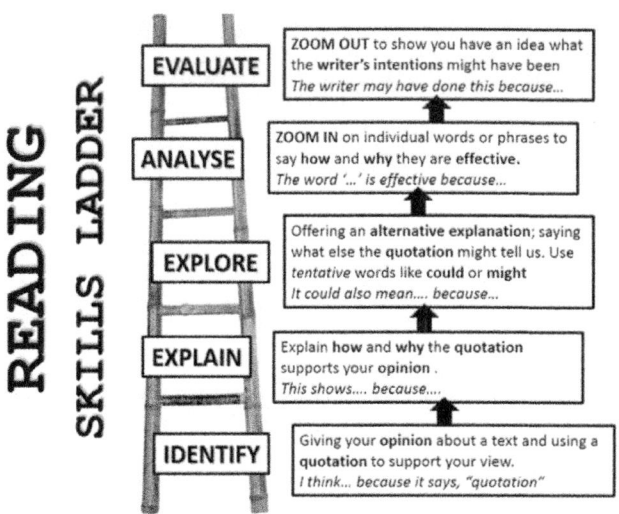

Understanding Point, Evidence, and Explanation (PEE)

Zoom (analyze)

After our explanation, comes zoom. Imagine zooming in and out with a camera. You zoom in to view the delicate parts of the picture, and you zoom out to view the image as a whole. Zoom is a much bigger analysis. You can zoom in on one word or phrase, in particular, discussing it in detail (take a look at the above ladder to see how you can introduce zoom). You can either zoom in or zoom out.

When you zoom in, you look at the fine details of individual words carefully and put each word under a microscope. Zooming in focuses on a brief, yet essential moment in the text, it enlarges each word. When you zoom out, you are analyzing your evidence as a whole.

> **Note:** An example of this is found within GCSE Language Paper 1. You will normally be asked to zoom in on specific parts of the extract given (usually questions 1, 2 and 4) and zoom out in other questions (question 3).

For example,

"Read again the first part of the source, from lines 1 to 4.

List four things about...from this part of the source."

And,

"Focus box this part of your answer on the second part of the source, from line 25 to

Understanding Point, Evidence, and Explanation (PEE)

the end.

A student said, '....'

To what extent do you agree?

In your response, you could:

- *consider your own impressions of ...*
- *evaluate how the writer conveys...*
- *support your response with references to the text."*

Zooming in and out is important because it tells the examiner that as much as you can analyze in close detail, you know how each word relates to each other, and how each word drives on the point you are trying to make. When zooming, you ask yourself these questions: how do I see each word? (zooming in)

- How does each word prove my point? (zooming in)
- What does the sentence as a whole mean? (zooming out)
- Interpret your words and connect them to one another

The basic idea of zooming is linking how small parts of a whole helps us to understand the entire extract or source. You'll develop your point in full depth when zooming – a very good way to raise your level within GCSE English.

Let's have a look at an example below:

I believe if you mismanage time, you are likely to regret it. This shown when Tom, a college student exclaimed after seeing his test results, "Had it been I made proper use of time, I would never have failed this badly." We can see from the text that the

Understanding Point, Evidence, and Explanation (PEE)

action had already taken place in the past. Tom was expressing his regrets for a past action. His first phrase "Had it been" shows that Tom was considering what could have happened if he had made proper use of time and he concluded that he would never have failed that badly. The author may have used these words to show us Tom feels a great sense of regret, shame and perhaps even despair at the misuse of his time.

Here is another example below:

In the extract, we learn her Mum loves pies. This is clear when she finished eating a pie this morning, and she exclaimed: "Oh, pies are the best." A jovial tone can be deduced from her exclamation: "Oh," which means eating pies brings her delight. The remaining part of her exclamation, "pies are the best" signifies her love for pies and her silent request for another one. **By using the word "Oh,"** *the readers can detect sincerity in the words that follow the initial words, and we can create an image in our mind of the pleasure her Mum felt when finishing off the pie.*

The above examples use the zooming feature (in bold). It zooms into the evidence to fully support the point it has already made. It zooms into the specific words and zooms out to bring in those words to support their point.

Getting up to 'Analyse' (Zoom) on the ladder shows you have a good grasp of how to use PEE to an effective standard but more importantly, how to write a paragraph to a high standard.

Understanding Point, Evidence, and Explanation (PEE)

However, in your PEE response, you should look to wrap this up nicely by completing the 'Evaluate' section. As shown in the ladder, you can start off with a sentence such as, "The writer may have done this because..." This indicates that you have explained why the author/writer may have used this particular word and what they hope to achieve by using this (as shown in the examples).

Note: Whilst it is ideal to apply the zoom technique in each paragraph, it may not always be possible to zoom into a word much analysis. Don't worry, make sure you provide a strong, detailed explanation in which you cover feelings, attitudes and bringing in the context of the source.

Understanding Point, Evidence, and Explanation (PEE)

Things to consider before you start writing:

1. Know your topic: A background knowledge of your topic allows you to write effectively. How?
   - Gather sources and pieces of information
   - Read about your topic
   - Know what you are supposed to write about and the purpose of your essay i.e.

Role: Who are you as the writer? e.g., The editor for a student magazine? A concerned member of the public?

Audience: To whom are you writing, e.g., Your school friends? Your work colleagues?

Format: In what format are you writing, e.g., A diary? A tabloid newspaper?

2. Brainstorming: Brainstorm after getting the topic for reasons or points to support or illuminate the topic. How?
   - Write down your main idea
   - Write your reasons for your main idea
   - Highlight language features/structural devices you're going to talk about

3. Choosing points
   - Choose your three best reasons that support your main idea the best

Understanding Point, Evidence, and Explanation (PEE)

- Make sure they are different, so you do not have the same or very similar ideas
- Put the best three points and put them in order of importance, from least important to the most important.

> **Note:** Brainstorming ideas and making a list of your points before writing is beneficial to keep you on track and make sure you're not confused as you begin your writing. **Remember, examiners will reward you for showing brainstorming your ideas even if you do not complete your writing so don't miss out on the opportunity to plan your writing!**

Understanding Point, Evidence, and Explanation (PEE)

Writing

Opening Paragraph

Grab their attention! Whether you're writing for an article in a Broadsheet Newspaper or Diary entry, a key thing to remember with writing is making sure you capture the attention of readers. A slow start to your writing can be detrimental (just like in films), and your audience can quickly lose interest in the points to follow.

Here are some ways to begin your opening paragraph:

- Ask a provocative / rhetorical question
- Make a bold/shocking statement
- Provide a statistic/fact
- Tell a short story
- Define a term
- Create a verbal picture

Understanding Point, Evidence, and Explanation (PEE)

After your opening paragraph, PEE on it.

Point: Your reason or claim. (Refer to the earlier topics to look at how you can begin making your point).

Your points are synonymous with your topic sentences. They tell the reader what your paragraph will be discussing.

Evidence: Provide enough grounds for your claim.

Explanation: Justify your claims, i.e., explain how your evidence justifies the evidence given.

- It is the most time-consuming step
- It provides evidence for the explanation
- It supports your point/reasons from the topic sentence
- It gives details, clarifies and adds meaning
- It makes use of transactions such as 'by this I mean, to explain, this means that....'

Understanding Point, Evidence, and Explanation (PEE)

Writing an in-depth paragraph using PEE:

> **Task!**
> Cover the answer below, read the passage and answer the question below:

In Shakespeare's Othello, would you say Othello seduced Desdemona or fell in love with him of her own accord?

Answer:

In my opinion, Othello never seduced Desdemona; instead, she fell in love with him of her own accord. This can be seen in Desdemona's response to her father's accusation

"...but here's my husband, and so much duty as my mother show's to you, preferring you before her father."

These statements imply the extent of her sincere love for Othello, such that she was ready to profess it in her father's presence and even in front of the council.

The word "preferring" indicates a decision made in complete control by Desdemona as she considered her options and decided to choose Othello, whereas the word seduced signifies a lack of control or choice. Shakespeare may have done this to provide the impression Desdemona is a decisive and strong-willed lady who is unlikely to fall to the seduction techniques of a male, as she was willing to articulate her decision in front of

Understanding Point, Evidence, and Explanation (PEE)

those she may fear. Rather, it is assumed she has a sound understanding of what she wants – in this case Othello, and she's even willing to challenge the norms of society to get what she wants.

Analysis:

In the answer above, we can see the question (point) being answered straightaway, "Othello never seduced Desdemona". This clarifies for the examiner your opinion on the question. Try to make sure you answer the question within the opening one or two lines.

In the second line, the evidence is introduced, "This can be seen in...". The evidence is a little longer than usual but if the language is difficult to understand, it may be useful to add a few more words within your evidence.

"These statements imply" begins the explanation. This is a short sentence and obvious answer that can be interpreted from the text. Whilst this sentence shows you understand the basics of the passage, simply answering up to this point will not show you have a comprehensive understanding of the text.

Next, we begin to develop our answer by zooming in on a word "preferring". We comment further on why this is an effective word used by Shakespeare and how this supports our viewpoint.

Finally, we zoom out, reflect further on the character of Desdemona and contextualize our answer. Now, we have discussed in detail about the type of person Desdemona was and why we can strongly believe she was not seduced by Othello.

Understanding Point, Evidence, and Explanation (PEE)

Points to consider when writing an essay:

1. The main body of the essay

The rest of your essay is an explanation of each of your point summarized in paragraph one.

Every point will have its own paragraph; each paragraph will include its own P.E.E

P - Point you are making in that paragraph.

E - Evidence to support your point.

E - Explanation of the evidence raised.

2. Structure

A simple essay should have an introduction, four or five paragraphs, each containing one central point and a conclusion.

A Paragraph is a miniature composition (compositions in a small form). It contains a topic sentence which is developed in that paragraph. The significant ideas are further explained through supporting sentences.

Paragraph unity: This means that only one important idea is discussed in a paragraph. Every paragraph, therefore, contains a key sentence or a keyword which is the subject of the paragraph, i.e., the sentence or word that all other sentences in a paragraph describe, discuss or explain.

Understanding Point, Evidence, and Explanation (PEE)

Coherence: This entails that a writer should discuss ideas in a particular order that readers can follow.

Cohesion: In cohesion, sentences together must hang together, i.e., each sentence must be connected to the preceding or following one in the same paragraph. No paragraph should stand alone. Transitional words or linkers can also be used such as 'also, similarly, but, on the other hand, in contrast, meanwhile, during the period, hence, therefore, in summary.' Avoid words like 'summarily' and 'conclusively.'

> **Note:** Each paragraph needs its structure (PEE). State your point, back it up with a piece of evidence and then explain it.

Understanding Point, Evidence, and Explanation (PEE)

Where else can we use PEE Paragraphs?

PEE paragraphs can be used when you are reading a book in class.

Point - raise a crucial aspect of a passage or chapter, e.g., emotion or feeling.

Evidence - pick a quote from the text or an observation

Explanation - explain what the quotation or observation means.

> **Note:** If your quotation is just a few words then you can put it inside a sentence in your paragraph. If you are quoting a more extended passage (like three or four lines of poetry, description or dialogue), then you should leave a line and indent the whole quotation, so it sits in the middle of the page.

Also, you may use PEE Paragraphs when:

- Discussing the language techniques and features used by a writer – this is usually found within a GCSE Language Paper 1. For example,

    "How does the writer use language here to convey...? You could include the writer's choice of:
    - words and phrases
    - language features and techniques
    - sentence forms"

Understanding Point, Evidence, and Explanation (PEE)

- Elaborating on structural features found within an insert – this has also been a regular feature in recent years within the GCSE Language Paper 1.

  "How has the writer structured the text to interest you as a reader?

  You could write about:
  - what the writer focuses your attention on at the beginning of the source
  - how and why the writer changes this focus as the source develops
  - any other structural features that interest you."

- Presenting how an author portrays a particular theme or relationship – typically, we can expect to find a question testing this skill in the GCSE Literature Paper 1.

  "Starting with this conversation, explore how…presents the romantic relationship of…

  Write about:
  - how…presents the romantic relationship at this moment in the play
  - how…presents the romantic relationship in the play as a whole"

We see that many questions within the GCSE Literature and Language will test your ability to write to an optimum level. Of course, examiners are not testing your ability to write a PEE paragraph using this method, but your skills to express yourself in the form of a paragraph.

Understanding Point, Evidence, and Explanation (PEE)

Using PEE to talk about language features and techniques:

You will be repeatedly asked about the language used by writers within GCSE English. This may be within exams as mentioned earlier, alongside the classroom, so it's useful to know how to apply PEE in these situations.

Let's remind ourselves how we may be tested on language features by looking at this sample question...

Look in detail at this extract, from lines 9 to 15 of the source:

"Mr Walsh remembered a time – surely, not so long ago – when books were golden, when imaginations soared, when the world was filled with stories which ran like gazelles and pounced like tigers and exploded like rockets, illuminating minds and hearts. He had seen it happen; had seen whole classes swept away in the fever. In those days, there were heroes; there were dragons and dinosaurs; there were space adventurers and soldiers of fortune and giant apes. In those days, thought Mr Walsh, we dreamed in colour, though films were in black and white, and good always triumphed in the end."

"How does the writer use language here to convey Mr. Walsh's views on books and stories of the past? You could include the writer's choice of:

*- words and phrases
- language features and techniques
- sentence forms" (8 marks)*

Understanding Point, Evidence, and Explanation (PEE)

Answer:

The writer has used adventurous imagery word throughout the extract. The word, "heroes" illustrates a romanticized view that Mr. Walsh holds of the past. As readers, we can interpret Mr. Walsh to have a nostalgic view to books he's read in the past – giving authors the roles of idols. As such, he seems to have a blinkered view of intelligent, modern literature and this prevents him from recognizing original interpretations to creativity and writing within literature. We further see this through the alliteration used, "dragons and dinosaurs". This demonstrates his view of the authors being superheroes who can do little wrong, with even a possession of divine attributes. Subsequently, moving onto contemporary writings would be a real challenge for him and therefore he would have a minute appreciation for the efforts of his students.

Also, the writer focuses on light imagery within the extract to convey Mr. Walsh's views on stories of the past. The metaphor "illuminating minds and hearts" has been used with great effect to demonstrate how the books brightened the students intellectually and thereby giving them a broadened understanding of literature. By using the word, "illuminating", the writer is encouraging us to think the students were in darkness, and perhaps even lost and in need of rescuing.

The writer again alludes to the idea of light imagery with the use of, "dreamed in colour". In the mind of Mr. Walsh, thinking about books of the past has always been sunny, colourful and even adventurous.

Understanding Point, Evidence, and Explanation (PEE)

Checking first drafts of work:

Work must always be planned and sometimes re-drafted completely. Even in an exam situation, make sure your explanation flows nicely and where possible, linked to the next paragraph.

- Check thoroughly (it's helpful if you can get someone to read it through for you)
- Check for punctuation errors (especially full stops and capital letters)
- Check for spelling errors
- Look for other ways to improve your first draft, e.g. the vocabulary you use, the ways you express ideas
- Check and confirm that you have answered the question correctly
- Check your paragraph structure. Have you used PEE and followed the PEE ladder?
- Is there an introduction, body and a conclusion?

> **Task!**
> Cover the answer below, read the following passage and answer the question that follows:

"Kate loves her class teacher so much. Not only because she explains her subjects so well but because Kate sees her as a role model. Ever since Kate was given birth to, her aspiration has always been to graduate with a good result and become a teacher, just like her class teacher. Kate sees her class teacher

Understanding Point, Evidence, and Explanation (PEE)

as a role model. She goes to her for pieces of advice, she shops for dresses that make her appear smart anytime she goes to the mall with her parents. She takes a keen interest in her studies and continuously accepts correction as when due."

Question:

Why does Kate love her class teacher?

Answer:

It's clear from the passage that Kate loves her class teacher because she sees her as a role model. I know this because it says, "Ever since Kate was given birth to, her aspiration has always been to graduate with a good result and become a teacher, just like her class teacher." The above suggests the extent to which Kate adores her class teacher. Kate sees her class teacher as a role model and hopes to be someone like her one day.

The words, "given birth to" indicates that Kate has been interested in academia and succeeding in life with a strong education from a very early age and has not considered doing anything else. The author may have used these words, so the readers sense the significance of graduating to Kate and how the idea of being well educated has been with her prior to her attending this class. It may also cause the readers to feel that becoming a teacher is part of Kate's destiny and therefore she will not stop until she succeeds in her education.

Understanding Point, Evidence, and Explanation (PEE)

Literature and Argument Essays

Literature or argument essays are pieces of writing where you present an argument - They must always have:

1. An introduction: introduce your essay topic
2. An argument: write a minimum of three or four paragraphs - depending on the essay
3. A conclusion: Give your most important arguments or an overview briefly - add no new ideas. The conclusion ties the essay together. It summarizes the salient points raised in an essay, drives home the points raised in earlier paragraphs and links them to the same theme.

Each paragraph of the argument must make use of PEE.

Point - This restates the question set in the title but focuses on one argument. This is the topic sentence.

Evidence - This is the evidence - quotation, facts or other viewpoints.

Explain -

- Why did it happen?
- What do you think about it?
- How did it make you/the readers feel?
- What does it tell you about the character?

Understanding Point, Evidence, and Explanation (PEE)

> **Task!**
> Cover the answer below, read the following dialogue and answer the question that follows:

Mabel: Hey Johnson. Have you seen my notebook?

Johnson: No.

Mabel: Do you mind helping me to look for it? I need it so badly. My mum checks my note each time I get back from school, and she must not find out that my note is missing.

Johnson: What are you going to do now?

Mabel: I honestly have no idea.

Question:

Looking at the extract above, why do you think Mabel badly wants to get her notebook back?

Answer:

It is clear from the extract Mabel wants to get her notebook back because she doesn't want her mum to find out about the missing note. This can be seen in her statement to Johnson, "My mum checks my note each time I get back from school, and she must not find out that my note is missing." This statement implies that the only reason she's looking for her note is that she doesn't want her mum to find out, perhaps because of the

Understanding Point, Evidence, and Explanation (PEE)

punishment that might be lashed out to her if her mum ever finds out.

The words "each time" is an indication Mabel's mum is an authoritarian and likes to keep a close eye on the movements of Mabel. This is further supported by "so badly" which illustrates the fear within Mabel of her mum.

The author's intentions are to create a sense of panic as this is demonstrated with Mabel's final comment of "I honestly have no idea". This makes us feel the fear emanating from Mabel as she's unsure how she's going to handle the situation of the missing note.

Understanding Point, Evidence, and Explanation (PEE)

Short essay using the PEE:

In the below example, you can see how the PEE method can still be applied to a free writing task which tests your creative skills. Whilst you may not have a text to look at, you can always follow the PEE method to formulate and structure a comprehensive response to a question testing your creative abilities.

SELF CONFIDENCE - A NECESSARY KEY TO SUCCESS

It is clear from the quietly confident doctor whose advice we rely on, to the charismatic confidence of an inspiring speaker, self-confident people have qualities that everyone admires. This can be seen in situations where nobody wants to partner in a deal that was struck by one who is nervous, fumbling and overly apologetic. However, one may be easily persuaded by someone who speaks very clearly, holds his or her head high, answers questions assuredly and who readily admits when he or she does not know something. This is so as confident people inspire confidence in others: their audience, partners, bosses, colleagues, customers, and friends.

Similarly, how you feel about yourself is a crucial issue in achieving anything in life. For example, if you do not have confidence in yourself and abilities, how can you expect others to? When attending job interviews, defending a project, bidding on an item, the way you behave and believe in yourself will ultimately create a win or lose situation. This reveals that self-confidence denotes believing in oneself and one's powers, skills or abilities. It is that unexplainable and untouchable attribute that allows you to get in touch with that inner self which enables you to express yourself adequately. Self-confidence doesn't increase overnight; you can only build it up to the level of your aspiration.

In my opinion, setting achievable goals is a key ingredient to building self-confidence. For example, do not expect perfection in your first attempt. Progress, not perfection is the attitude that builds confidence. "Just do it!" Be gentle with yourself and don't put yourself down if you make a mistake. If you are afraid of something, do it anyway. Most times, fear disappears when we face the things we are scared of.

Another way of boosting your self-confidence is socializing with self-confident people and spending time in suitable environments. This is because the people around you affect your confidence level, so seek the company of those who are confident and honest with you. Try to avoid negative people, as they can pull you down. Identify your negative thoughts and turn them into positive thoughts; this might take positive affirmations such as "I can do this." Start with a few positive thoughts a day.

Similarly, the smallest things can improve self-confidence. This can be demonstrated when you add a smile when making a phone call, and it will show in your voice. Straightening posture or giving a warm handshake returns a positive response. Making eye contacts conveys self-confidence. Stop comparing yourself to others. Take pride in yourself, keep a list of your achievements. This will keep you motivated.

Understanding Point, Evidence, and Explanation (PEE)

In conclusion, without confidence, you will never venture out of your comfort zone.

Analysis of SELF CONFIDENCE – A NECESSARY KEY TO SUCCESS:

The first paragraph, which is the introductory paragraph starts firstly by stating a point, goes ahead to give evidence and explanation. The paragraph is followed by subsequent paragraphs following the same pattern.

Each PEE chain starts with pointers such as for the points; we have points, e.g. "In my opinion," "Similarly." When explaining, we have pointers such as "For example," "An example of this is."

Lastly, when giving the evidence, a pointer like "this is because", is used. The use of this chain makes the essay flow smoothly as well as making it easier to read.

Understanding Point, Evidence, and Explanation (PEE)

Final Note:

This short guide has been compiled to guide students studying GCSE English. Noticing a distinct lack of support and conduct for students outside the classroom when it comes to PEE, I have attempted to put together many of the ideas taught by teachers within secondary schools today.

For years, mastering the teaching of the PEE method has been the focus of English teachers and knowing how to execute this effectively has been the cause of stress and tension for students. I hope this small compilation of PEE notes goes a long way to supporting you as students to understand this vital concept of Point, Evidence, Explanation and thereby allowing you to succeed with your creative writing.

Understanding Point, Evidence, and Explanation (PEE)

About the author:

Lana Davies is a certified Teacher with years of experience within the classroom teaching GCSE English. Lana has spent a number of years teaching Key Stage 3 and 4 students using the Point, Evidence, Explanation method using a variety of powerful techniques.